The Diary of
DAVID R. LEEPER
Rushing for Gold

edited by Connie and Peter Roop

illustrations and map by Laszlo Kubinyi

BENCHMARK BOOKS

MARSHALL CAVENDISH
NEW YORK

For our Canadian readers, and any others who use the metric system, here is a quick conversion table to help you with the weights and measures used in this book.

Area
1 square foot = 0.093 square meters
1 acre = 4,047 square meters

Distance
1 foot = 30.48 centimeters
1 mile = 1.6 kilometers

Capacity
1 keg = 30 gallons = 136.4 liters

Weight
1 ounce = 28.350 grams
1 pound = 453.59 grams
1 ton = 2,000 pounds = 0.907 metric tons

Benchmark Books
Marshall Cavendish Corporation
99 White Plains Road
Tarrytown, New York 10591-9001
Illustrations and map copyright © 2001 by Marshall Cavendish Corp.
Text copyright © 2001 by Connie and Peter Roop

Library of Congress Cataloging-in-Publication Data
Leeper, David Rohrer, 1832–1900.
The diary of David R. Leeper : Rushing for gold / edited by Connie and Peter Roop.
    p.   cm.— (In my own words)
Includes bibliographical references and index.
Summary: A young prospector describes his experiences traveling overland to
the California gold fields and during the five years he spent digging for gold.
ISBN 0-7614-1011-2 (lib.bdg.)
1.Leeper, David Rohrer, 1832–1900—Diaries—Juvenile literature. 2. California—Gold
discoveries—Juvenile literature. 3. Pioneers—California—Diaries—Juvenile literature.
4. Frontier and pioneer life—California—Juvenile literature. 5. Overland journeys to the
Pacific—Juvenile literature. 6. Frontier and pioneer life—West (U.S.)—Juvenile literature.
[1. Leeper, David Rohrer, 1832–1900. 2. Pioneers. 3. Gold mines and mining. 4. California—
Gold discoveries. 5. Frontier and pioneer life—California. 6. Diaries.] I. Roop, Connie.
II. Roop, Peter. III. Title. IV. In my own words (Benchmark Books (Firm))
F865.L485   2000   979.4'04—dc21   00-023840

Printed in Hong Kong
3   5   6   4   2

For Tom and Terri Loveall,
who have hearts of gold

Leeper's Book

THE

ARGONAUTS OF 'FORTY-NINE

SOME RECOLLECTIONS OF THE PLAINS AND THE DIGGINGS

BY

DAVID ROHRER LEEPER

ILLUSTRATED

BY O. MARION ELBEL, FROM SELECTIONS AND SUGGESTIONS

BY THE AUTHOR

"Golden days, remembered days,
The days of 'Forty-Nine"

SOUTH BEND, INDIANA
J. B. STOLL & COMPANY, PRINTERS
1894

THE TITLE PAGE OF DAVID LEEPER'S BOOK

INTRODUCTION

On January 24, 1848, James Marshall found gold at Sutter's Mill in California. It was supposed to be kept secret, but word of his discovery leaked to the outside world. By the following year, a stampede of humanity was making its way to California. The gold rush was on!

Some gold seekers came to California by ship around Cape Horn, the southern tip of South America. Others traveled to Panama and Nicaragua, crossed from the Atlantic to the Pacific Ocean, and continued their journey to California. Most people rushing for gold traveled overland across America, a journey filled with hardship, danger, and adventure.

Who were these nineteenth-century Argonauts, these gold hunters? Most were men, although women and children sometimes made the journey. Word of the great fortunes to be made in the gold-fields lured people from all walks of life — teachers, shopkeepers, clerks, doctors, lawyers, farmers — everyone, in short, who wished to get rich quick.

Three weeks after the discovery of gold at Sutter's Mill, California became a territory of the United States. California had been acquired as a result of the American victory over Mexico in the Mexican-American War (1846–1848). At that time no one knew of the wealth hidden beneath its rocks and rivers. California was not a highly populated place. Scattered throughout the region were ranchers and farmers as well as several tribes of Native Americans. The area, although warm and sunny, was not a popular destination for emigrants from the East. Most pioneers in 1848 headed for Oregon, not California.

The situation changed rapidly when gold was discovered. By September 9, 1850, enough people lived in California for it to become the thirty-first state. Its nickname quickly caught on: The Golden State.

Most Forty-niners, however, did not strike it rich. The dream of gold lying on the ground waiting to be picked up was just that, a dream. Digging for gold was hard, dirty work. The precious metal had to be panned from freezing rivers, dug out of the ground, or blasted out. As a popular song said:

"They told us of the heaps of dust,
And the lumps so mighty big.
But they never said a single word
How hard it was to dig!"

As more and more miners arrived, prices for food, clothing, equipment, and shelter soared. Potatoes cost a dollar apiece. One box of sardines was sixteen dollars. Frequently, the only people who got rich were the shopkeepers, saloonkeepers, and boardinghouse owners.

Living conditions were often terrible. Men slept in leaky tents and crowded cabins. Some slept under the open sky. Fights, robberies, and murders frequently occurred.

Many Forty-niners returned home disillusioned and disappointed. But many more stayed on, becoming farmers, ranchers, loggers, builders, railroad workers, teachers, cooks, businesspeople, bankers. Together, they built the foundation of the California we know today.

Few of the eager gold seekers took time to write accounts of their journey west or of the time they spent digging for gold. One who did was David R. Leeper, who was a young man when he set out from Indiana in February 1849. His journey across the continent took months and was filled with adventure and hardship, excitement and danger. After he finally arrived in California, he spent years struggling to strike it rich. He was forced to fall back on his trade as

DAVID LEEPER, FROM A PHOTOGRAPH TAKEN WHEN HE WAS AN OLDER MAN

woodsman, chopping down trees, in order to earn his keep and continue digging for gold.

Leeper did find gold, but just enough to keep him going, not enough to make his fortune. He returned home in 1854. His years working the goldfields were not a complete loss, however, for he later turned his hand to writing. Thanks to his account, we can see for ourselves, 150 years later, what it was like to be part of the great California Gold Rush.

Here, then, in his own words, is David Leeper's story.

—Connie and Peter Roop
Appleton, Wisconsin

The Diary of David R. Leeper
Rushing for Gold

Ho, for Sacramento

On February 22, 1849, our party of six set out
from South Bend, Indiana, for the newly discovered goldfields of California. We were William
Good, Michael Donahue, Thomas Rockhill,
William Earl, Thomas Neal, and me, the writer,
David Leeper. We were young: the oldest
twenty-five, the youngest seventeen.

Our equipment consisted of two wagons, seven
yoke of oxen, and two years' supplies. The long
journey before us, the unknown region through
which it lay, and the glamour of the object for
which it was undertaken, lent our adventure
considerable local interest. Many friends and
spectators were present to witness our departure.
Our two covered wagons were objects of much
curious concern as they rolled out of town with
two thousand miles of wilderness before them.

For us the occasion had few pangs. The gold
diggings had been discovered but a twelve-month
before. The glowing tales of the marvelous riches

were on every tongue. Our enthusiasm was wrought up to the highest pitch. The hardships and perils of such a journey were scarcely given a passing thought. Several parties of our acquaintance had already gone before us. Others were preparing to go, which further intensified our eagerness.

It was therefore with light hearts, and perhaps lighter heads, that we lustily joined in the chorus of the inspiring ditty of the time:

"Oh, California!
That's the land for me.
I am going to Sacramento
With my washbowl on my knee!"

In 1849 the West was still very new. Even Chicago had not heard the whistle of the locomotive. Illinois, Iowa, and Missouri were, for the most part, an unbroken prairie with ten to twenty miles between neighbors. The cooing of prairie chickens filled the air like the roar of a distant waterfall. The grasslands were strewn with antlers of deer and elk, attesting to the abundance of this game.

Westward of Iowa and Missouri, the vast area of mountains and plains stretched away to where the surf beat of the Pacific laves the golden shore. This region was laid down on maps as *Terra Incognita*, the Unknown Land. Except at three or four isolated spots, where a mission or military post had been set up, not an abode of the white man was to be seen.

This was the land we were determined to cross to reach our goal: California or bust!

Not a Holiday Junket

We were not long in finding out that the adventure meant more than poetry and romance.

We left home in the midst of a thaw and from the very start were beset with mud. We were frequently compelled to make wide detours, avoiding the roads, so as to escape the floods and bottomless lowlands. Added to the difficulties of travel were the inconveniences suffered from the scantiness of accommodations for ourselves and our animals.

William Good and William Earl sported better clothes than their companions. On starting upon the journey, Good wore a silk hat and Earl a swallowtail coat. The hat soon became battered. One sleeve of the coat was chewed into pulp up to the elbow by an ox, but Earl continued to wear the garment proudly.

The irksomeness of the journey was somewhat relieved by our naturally buoyant party. We were able to muster several musical instruments:

WE LEFT HOME IN THE MIDST OF A THAW AND FROM THE VERY START WERE BESET WITH MUD.

violin, banjo, tambourine, and castanets. We were all backwoods vocal virtuosos. Singing and playing, we whiled away many an evening by our campfires, which otherwise would have dragged heavily on our hands. In fact, our musical fame spread far and near along our route. It won us the reputation of being the wildest and jolliest lot of Hoosiers ever let loose outside the hoop pole and pumpkin state.

Hoosier (HOO-zhur) a nickname for a resident of Indiana

Camp experience was by no means conducive to sweetness of temper. In fact, it was a common remark that men were decidedly more irascible on the plains than they had been at home, not infrequently culminating in hot words and sometimes in blows.

St. Joseph, Missouri, was our objective point on the frontier. We found this border city, the last outpost of civilization, thronged with gold seekers like ourselves. They had flocked hither from every quarter for the overland journey. Many had pushed out before our arrival. Many were still coming in and all was hurry-scurry with excitement.

The only transportation available for crossing the Missouri River was a big clumsy flatboat propelled by long oars. We chartered this craft for one night with several other parties, and our wagons rolled onboard. The price stipulated was ninety dollars, and we were to perform the labor. The task was by no means a holiday diversion! I tugged at one of those oars myself all night long, and it seemed a long, long night indeed.

Adieu to Civilization!

On May 16, we pulled from the Missouri River
through the muddy timbered bottom to the open
bluffs. We had now bid adieu to civilization.
Some fifteen hundred miles lay before us. Many
emigrants were encamped about us. We were,
therefore, not long in marshaling a train of some
sixty wagons equipped with officers and a
bristling code of rules. Guards were to pass
their beats regularly and the animals were all to
be carefully corralled at night by arranging the
wagons into a circle.

As we pushed out from the river bluffs into
the open country beyond, our long line of
"prairie schooners" looked sightly as it gracefully
wound itself over the green billowy landscape.
But, as we found out, our thing of beauty was
not to be a joy forever as you will see.

We had not been out many days when I
discovered a good wagon tire. Such reckless

Prairie Schooners

The covered wagons that carried the gold seekers across America got the name *prairie schooners* because, from a distance, their white canvas tops looked like the sails of a ship. Prairie schooners were also used by pioneers making the long journey to the West Coast. It took some four to six months to travel from Independence, Missouri, to Oregon or California.

The wagons were pulled by teams of oxen or mules and could roll along at the rate of fifteen miles a day on a good day. To cross rivers, the wagons were either floated like boats or ferried over on flatboats or rafts. During the Gold Rush, at some locations along the overland trails, more than 450 prairie schooners could be seen rolling by each summer day.

Some wagons carried up to ten tons of supplies. As David Leeper learned to his dismay, such heavy burdens could not be carried very long. The travelers were often forced to drop their supplies along the way as the animals grew weary.

Patriotic gold seekers often painted their wagon frames blue and the wheels red, keeping their canvas tops white. Sometimes they painted slogans on the sides, such as "California or Bust."

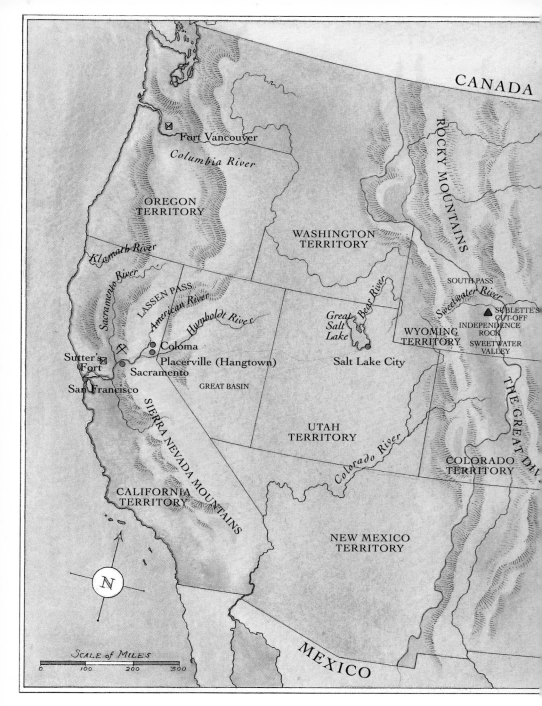

DAVID LEEPER'S RUSH FOR GOLD TOOK HIM ACROSS THE GREAT AMERICAN
WEST. IN 1849 THE WEST WAS STILL NEW. LEEPER JOURNEYED OVER
PRAIRIES AND DESERTS, MOUNTAINS AND RIVERS TO REACH THE FABLED
GOLDFIELDS OF CALIFORNIA.

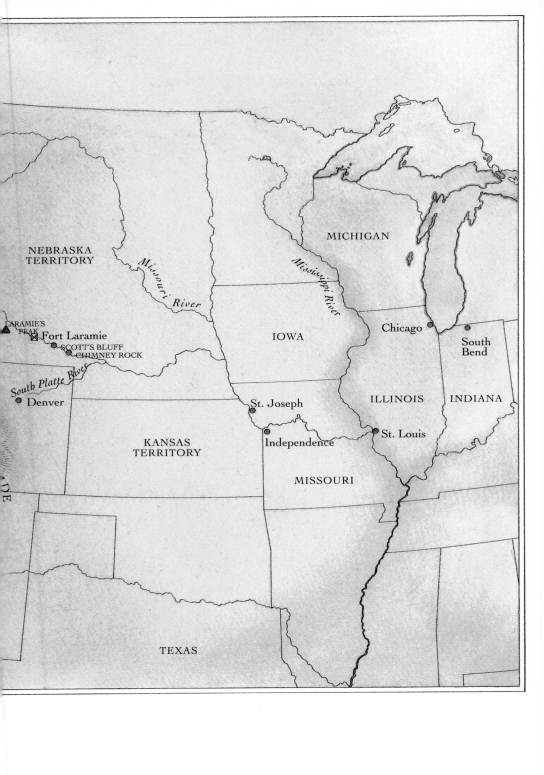

abandonment of property was something new to me. I stopped to acquire it.

I rolled the valuable article for a while, striving to catch up to the moving wagon train. But I soon had to abandon the wheel in despair.

From this time onward, we saw castaway articles strewn by the roadside in increasing profusion. Tons and tons of bacon and other articles were burned to lighten the loads. Many emigrants had provided enough supplies to last them a year or two. But they were not long in reducing their load as much as possible for both their teams and their progress. Even so, some draft animals perished, some stampeded, and all became foot-worn.

Fuel for our cooking fires was quite an object through that part of the route now known as Nebraska and eastern Wyoming. Weeds and buffalo "chips" were about the only resource. The latter made an excellent fuel when it could be had. To cook we improvised a furnace by cutting a narrow trench in the ground so the coffeepot and frying pan could span the breadth of the fire and rest upon the walls of the opening. Coffee, flapjacks, and bacon were about the only articles we prepared. In the "flipping" of the flapjacks we soon were very expert!

As to our grand caravan, it steadily came to grief. As we approached the mountains, the rough roads and difficult passages delayed progress by the necessity of one team having to wait on another. Some wagons went on ahead while others fell behind. Some dropped out completely.

Our own little party underwent depletions from time to time until but three members of the original six remained. Now my only companions from home were Thomas Rockhill and Thomas Neal. We abandoned our tents early as useless luxuries. Instead, each of us sought out the most eligible site he could find (usually among the sagebrush) and rolled himself up in his blankets and buffalo robes with only the starry canopy for a shelter.

Near where we would ford the South Fork of the Platte River we had the good fortune to come upon a large village of Sioux, who were in the locality. These Indians struck me as being decidedly comely: neat, healthy, self-poised. Their dress was made chiefly of white-tanned skins, and they looked very picturesque in their elaborate decorations of beadwork and other adornments.

Game was by no means as plentiful as one would have supposed. We found more of it in the states through which we had passed than in the country beyond. In the region now known as Nebraska, many antelopes were seen bounding over the plain or watching our movements from elevated points. But they were shy, vigilant, and hard to capture. In the mountains, deer and mountain sheep were occasionally sighted and brought down. On the whole, our banquets on the luxuries of the chase were few and far between. Strange to say, we saw but few buffaloes, not more than a dozen or so, all told.

We forded the South Fork of the Platte. It was, at our place of crossing, a broad, shallow stream, with a treacherous quicksand bottom. From this branch of the Platte, our trail lay over a high, open, rolling country, via Ash Hollow, for a distance of about fifty miles, to the North Fork of the Platte. We then followed the course of the latter stream some three hundred miles. The country now gradually increased in ruggedness, thus heralding our approach toward the Rocky Mountains.

Illusions of the Land

The cliffs and highlands along the Platte became objects of special interest. These cliffs were in many instances wrought into various forms that appeared to be artistic creations, such as churches, castles, towers, embattlements, and architectural ruins.

The presence of cacti and other arid-loving plants assured us that we were treading the soil of the so-called arid region. The villages of the prairie dog had become numerous, and the queer antics of this shy, vigilant, nimble, barking marmot afforded us much amusement. The stately owl and the lazy rattlesnake were constant but doubtless unwelcome copartners with the prairie dogs in the occupancy of these villages.

Court House Rock and Chimney Rock were among the more conspicuous of natural curiosities. Both were visible for a considerable distance. Ahead, in the direction we were going, the spire

Native Americans and the Forty-niners

The Forty-niners and other pioneers rarely encountered Native Americans as they rolled west across the continent. Tales of Indian attacks were largely rumors, although at times the native peoples did attack a wagon train passing through their territory. If an attack was anticipated, the travelers rolled their wagons into a defensive circle and placed their animals in the center, where they would be out of harm's way.

of Chimney Rock was peeping invitingly over the intervening hills.

It would be easy enough, to all appearances, to step over the Court House and cut across to Chimney Rock. The distance appeared so trifling as to give us no concern.

Well, the upshot was, that we did not reach Court House Rock until sundown. We hurriedly carved our names upon the walls. Then it required two and a half days' journeying before we stood under the shadow of Chimney Rock! Objects here on the plains appeared but a mile or two away when in reality they were often from five to ten. Even the stars seemed to steal down from their depths and look vastly nearer, greater, and grander.

About fifteen miles past Chimney Rock lay Scotts Bluffs. These high, picturesque escarpments had been occupying our attention for several days. These cliffs fell abruptly into the Platte, necessitating a circuit of some thirty miles across the uplands to bypass them.

We now began to catch an occasional glimpse of the outer and higher peaks of the Rocky Mountains. Laramie's Peak was the first of these to greet us. In a few days we passed Fort Laramie. The road had become rougher and the soil more parched. But the change was hailed as a welcome relief from the long-continued monotony of the plains. We had actually grown weary of good roads and sighed for something to shake us up. Another welcome change was the abundance of fuel, and the numerous mountain streams of pure cold water. We here made our first acquaintance with the sagebrush that was thenceforward to be our chief reliance for fuel.

EVEN THE STARS SEEMED TO STEAL DOWN FROM THEIR DEPTHS AND LOOK
VASTLY NEARER, GREATER, AND GRANDER.

The Rocky Mountains

From the appearance of the specimens before us, the name *rocky* seemed to have been readily enough suggested. The entire mass in sight was of primitive rock, wholly bare and destitute of vegetation except for a few stunted trees or shrubs.

Independence Rock was our first noted landmark. We celebrated the Fourth of July here. The rock took its name from a similar celebration that took place here years before by other travelers passing this way.

Our course now lay along the valley of the Sweetwater River for about one hundred miles to the South Pass, where we were to cross the Great Divide that separates the waters of the Atlantic and Pacific Oceans.

As we approached the divide, we observed several patches of snow near the roadside. Wildflowers were blooming close by these lingering relics of winter, thus attesting to the aptitude of Nature to respond to any environment, whatever its character. When upon the summit's South Pass, we were 7,490 feet above sea level and about six hundred miles from our point of departure on the frontier at St. Joseph, Missouri. We were halfway to California!

Just beyond South Pass we encamped at Pacific Springs, where for the first time we looked upon the water flowing Pacificward. The great Rocky Mountain range lay between us and home.

The Continental Divide

The Continental Divide is an imaginary line that winds its way down the length of the Rocky Mountains. The Continental Divide marks where water flows either east or west. The waters on the eastern side of the mountains eventually flow into the Mississippi River and down to the Gulf of Mexico. The waters on the western slopes run either to the Gulf of California by such rivers as the Green and Colorado or into the Pacific Ocean down the Snake and Columbia Rivers. Crossing the Continental Divide was a major goal for the Forty-niners.

A vast unknown region stretched away before us.

The trail at this point diverged, one branch going the way of the Great Salt Lake and the other by way of the Bear River. We took the latter branch, which was known as Sublette's Cut-off. Our road led directly through a small grove of tamarack, alder, and aspen trees, which crowned one of the more favored elevations. This grove was truly an enchanting spot; at least it so appeared to us after our thousand miles of timberless monotony.

The Bear River is the largest tributary of the Great Salt Lake. Here we saw our first and only geyser. The orifice or throat was about the size of a man's fist, and from this opening at rapid intervals a column of frothing steam and water was ejected into the air a number of feet. After each discharge the remaining water could be heard gurgling downward.

Near where we left the Bear River, we saw a band of Sho-sho-ne, or Snake, Indians. They were migrating nomad fashion, being mounted and carrying with them their families, many ponies, and all their equipments of the camp, the chase, and the warpath. The mounted braves; the fantastic trappings; the women with their

Geysers

Geysers are springs that throw up hot water with explosive force from time to time. You might call them water volcanoes. The vents, or openings, of most geysers are small, which causes the boiling water to shoot out with great force. The most famous geyser is Old Faithful in Yellowstone National Park (where there are dozens of different geysers), which erupts almost every hour.

burdens; the motley households; the pack ponies; the lodge poles dragging from the saddles of the ponies; the platform or litter here and there erected on these poles to convey the sick, disabled, and infirm; the whooping boys driving the loose ponies, all combined to form a most interesting panorama and one the like of which is never again to be witnessed in the wilds of this country.

We were now on the main Oregon emigrant trail. We usually carried a keg of water as a precaution. But the region through which we were

NEAR WHERE WE LEFT THE BEAR RIVER, WE SAW A BAND OF SHO-SHO-NE INDIANS.

passing was quite mountainous and afforded
water in such abundance that we began to think
it needless to exercise our usual practice of laying
in a supply.

It so happened on the very morning we had
neglected to fill our cask, we came upon a desert

The Oregon Trail

The Oregon Trail began in Independence,
Missouri, and wound two thousand miles
through prairies and deserts and across
mountains to the Pacific Northwest. It was
the longest route used in the westward
expansion of the United States. Thousands
of pioneer families traveled on the Oregon
Trail during the mid-1800s, seeking not the
riches of the goldfields but the fertile farm-
land of the Oregon Territory. The territory
later became the states of Washington and
Oregon. Many Forty-niners followed part
of the Oregon Trail. At South Pass, they
split off and headed south to California to
try to strike it rich.

stretch of forty miles! It was by far the most trying day's experience I had on the trip. Plodding on and on, stirred with alternating hope and disappointment upon every apparent change of landscape, toward the last I became so exhausted from thirst that I was compelled at frequent intervals to pause for a moment's rest and shelter. It is astonishing how long one, if driven to the test, will bear up when he would ordinarily think his last reserves are exhausted.

One day my curiosity led me to climb a high commanding eminence, and my toil was unexpectedly repaid with a fine view of the Great Salt Lake in the blue distance. Here and there streaks of dust on the intervening desert indicated the presence of plodding emigrant wagon trains on another route, as a streak of smoke on the ocean may indicate the presence of a steamer though nothing else than that streak may be seen.

Crossing a Wasteland

We were now in the heart of the arid wastes of the Great Basin, a region five hundred miles in width by eight hundred miles in length. We ran upon a party direct from the promised land, straight from the enchanting goldfields. The members of the group were quite communicative and gave us a flaming account of the diggings, backing up their words with a liberal display of the shining nuggets. This was the first real tangible proof we had of the existence of gold in California. Before we believed. Now we knew!

The effect was ravishing. It sent our spirits bounding up to the extreme limit of our mental barometers. An elderly member of our wagon train, upon viewing the yellow metal, could not restrain his enthusiasm. He capered about like an exuberant schoolboy. Shying his hat into the air, he shouted, "Glory Hallelujah! I'll be a rich man yet."

The Great Basin

After the Forty-niners passed over the Rocky Mountains they encountered the Great Basin. This vast, arid region makes up much of today's Nevada, as well as parts of Utah, California, Idaho, Wyoming, and Oregon.

Travel through the Great Basin was difficult at best for the gold seekers. Water sources were few and far between. Men and animals suffered when they could not find freshwater. Sometimes, water was found, but it was so full of minerals or other contaminants that it was undrinkable.

Food was another problem, for little game could live in this desert region. If the Forty-niners did not have adequate supplies when they entered the Great Basin, they were in danger of perishing from hunger as well as thirst.

After crossing the Great Basin, the gold seekers faced yet another hurdle: they had to climb up and over the towering Sierra Nevada Mountains before reaching California.

In marked contrast with this little episode, the words of the plaintive ditty of the gold-miner came to my mind times many and oft:

plaintive
sad,
melancholy

"They told us of the heaps of dust,
And lumps so mighty big;
But they never said a single word
How hard it was to dig."

We took a lofty divide to be part of the Sierra Nevada range, beyond which lay California, the land of our dreams. Our group became impatient, now that we supposed ourselves so near. But, after surmounting what we thought to be the summit, lo! another and still more formidable ascent loomed grimly and tauntingly before us. When at length we reached the Lassen Pass, we found the altitude still but little diminished and the gradient very heavy and laborious.

This formidable mountain barrier crossed, we did indeed find a welcome change. The moisture-laden, life-giving breezes from the Pacific had wrought the transformation. The vast desert area, with its widespread, death-dealing desolation, was no longer present. Grass, water, and fuel were now abundant. We passed through miles upon miles of pine forests whose giant growths were a

WHEN AT LENGTH WE REACHED THE LASSEN PASS, WE FOUND THE ALTITUDE
BUT LITTLE DIMINISHED AND THE GRADIENT VERY HEAVY AND LABORIOUS.

source of constant surprise and admiration.

We were now on the California-Oregon wagon road and, in the course of a few days, we met another party from the diggings. Again we were favored with a rose-colored picture of the "chunks" so mighty big.

California!

At Lassen's Ranch, where Peter Lassen had erected a log cabin, he kept a small stock of staple goods. This was the first sign of civilization we had seen for many a day. It was a motley scene of emigrants, Indians, and old-time Californians who greeted our vision. Not far away flowed the poetic river, the Sacramento, of whose glittering golden sands we had sung upon leaving home.

Was this our journey's end? This the goal of our many weary days, weeks, and months of toil, privation, peril? The eleventh day of October! Yes, seven months and nineteen days since we began the journey.

There, surely enough, as the river current whirled the flaky particles over and over in the sunlight, were the dazzling sands of gold. But were these particles gold? Were these really the sands that we were to gather with washbowls on our knees? We wanted to believe, but were afraid to trust our senses. Gold!

Yes, the gold of fools. For it turned out that the bright flakes were simply scales of mica, mingled with other ingredients of granite.

We were still fifty to sixty miles from the point where we had decided to locate, Redding's Diggings. A landmark on this short journey was the great white dome of Mount Shasta. Rising directly in our front, and far overtopping all the other peaks within our scope of vision, it constantly commanded attention, though we were at no time less than eighty miles away.

Finally we pitched camp at Redding's Diggings. The goldfields lay at the extreme head of the Sacramento Valley, very nearly at the site of the present town of Redding.

These fields were known as "dry diggings," which meant that they were worked chiefly with pick and spoon. The diggings were, so far as our experience went, "panned out," decidedly "dry" indeed. During our week's trial, we averaged hardly a dollar a day to the man.

We—Thomas Rockhill, Thomas Neal, and myself—became thoroughly disgusted with our luck here: we were down to our last fifty cents. We heard that we could earn sixteen dollars per cord for chopping wood in Sacramento City.

All of us were accustomed to the woods and the ax, so we at once decided to head for Sacramento, about one hundred and seventy miles distant. There we could make enough money to continue our search for gold. Soon after starting out, however, my companions left me to strike out on their own. I went on alone.

At length, I reached the American River. Sacramento City lay on the bank opposite. It took my last two-bits for ferriage. Thus, wet and bedraggled, I entered Sacramento in a worse predicament than Doctor [Benjamin] Franklin when he entered Philadelphia, for I had no pennies for loaves as he had.

two-bits about twenty-five cents

The First
California Gold

The appearance of Sacramento City was truly unique. Nearly all the buildings were made of canvas tacked upon poles. All was intense bustle and excitement. Here, intermingled and jostling each other, were representatives from every quarter of the globe, all moved by the one engrossing purpose: gold!

Two miles east of the city was the famous Sutter's Fort, which up to that season had been the terminus of the only overland wagon trail entering California. For nearly a decade it had been the focal point for the American residents of the area. The fort was established by Captain John A. Sutter.

terminus
end of a
travel route

The wood-chopping project did not turn out as expected and I again set face for the mines. I headed for Coloma, where Sutter had a sawmill and gold was first discovered. It lay about fifty miles from Sacramento. I was, of course, still "tramping" it. At Shingle Springs, I paid a dollar for the privilege of lodging in a covered cart, in company with a barrel of pork. Gold was the universal currency, and scales were a fixture in every place of business.

My next halt was at the double-log house on the Sacramento-Coloma road. My chief occupation was chopping wood. I cut logs for houses at a dollar each and I cut firewood at five dollars per cord. Board was six dollars per day, the sumptuous fare consisting of bacon, beans, coffee, and musty, soggy, buggy, wormy bread. Flour was two dollars per pound, and a villainous article, most of it having made the voyage round Cape Horn heated in some ship's hold. Potatoes were eight dollars per pound, the chief use to which they were put was as a cure for scurvy [which they weren't]. Scurvy was a common complaint then.

The locality was in the very heart of the best diggings in California, but I did not know this at the time. I often picked up good-sized nuggets in the dooryard after a heavy rain. But it did not occur to any of us woodcutters to prospect for

John Sutter and His Mill

John Sutter was a friendly, ambitious, enthusiastic emigrant from Switzerland. He had once been a merchant but had failed in this occupation. After roaming around America in the 1840s, he settled in Mexico, where he became a citizen. The governor of Mexico gave Sutter fifty thousand acres of prime land at the junction of the Sacramento and American Rivers in California. (The region belonged to Mexico until 1848.) Here Sutter made a fortune farming, ranching, and selling goods. He called the place Sutter's Fort.

To provide lumber for his building projects, Sutter, in partnership with James Marshall, constructed a sawmill. They built their mill about fifty miles from Sutter's Fort on the South Fork of the American River. It was at this sawmill that James Marshall discovered gold on January 24, 1848.

diggings, either there or anywhere else in the flat of several acres nearby.

Coloma, as is well known, is located on the

South Fork of the American River. It is distinguished historically as the place where, on January 24, 1848, James W. Marshall made the gold discovery that set the world ablaze. Marshall discovered the gold at the Sutter sawmill. I saw the mill many times. It was an old-fashioned flutter wheel and was pounding away day and night while I knew it.

Marshall's discovery at the mill was not, it appears, the result of mere accident. The waterwheel had been set too low. The water was being let into the tailrace [a channel bringing water to power the sawmill] at night to cut the channel deeper so as to free the wheel. It was Marshall's custom to walk along the race in the morning, after the water had been shut off, to give his men directions in their work.

On the day previous to the discovery, a section of the bedrock in the race excited his curiosity. He remarked that he believed there was gold thereabouts, this belief being founded on the fact that he had noticed the "blossom of gold quartz." He had read that the presence of such quartz was a sign of gold.

So strong was he in this belief that he sent a man for a pan so he might make the test by

I SAW THE MILL MANY TIMES. IT WAS AN OLD-FASHIONED FLUTTER WHEEL
AND WAS POUNDING AWAY DAY AND NIGHT WHILE I KNEW IT.

washing some sand and gravel taken from the tailrace. The test was unsuccessful. But the failure did not satisfy Marshall.

"Well," he said to his attendant, "we will hoist the gates tonight and let in all the water we can, and tomorrow morning we will shut it off and come down here. I believe we will find gold or some other mineral." As he was a rather eccentric sort of man, no heed was paid to this seeming whim.

But Marshall was in a different frame of mind. The next morning at an unusually early hour someone was heard pounding at the mill. It was Marshall. He came up from the tailrace carrying his slouch hat in his arms and, setting it on the workbench, exclaimed: "Boys, I believe I have found a gold mine!"

At once the men gathered around, and sure enough in the top of his hat, the crown knocked in a little, was the pure stuff in small pieces or rather thin scales. All were convinced that it was gold, although no one had ever seen the metal before in its natural state. It was agreed by all hands that the discovery should be kept secret. But the news took wing in spite of precautions to the contrary. The public, however, was slow to believe, so that it was some time before the importance of the event came to be realized.

Striking It Rich?

The days soon found me at Hangtown, which took its suggestive name from the circumstances that three men, two Frenchmen and a Spaniard, were hanged here for robbery and murder. Hangtown was, at this period, one of the most important mining camps in the state. Claims were limited to fifteen feet square, so the miners did not work long in a place.

The best diggings I struck were on Hangtown Creek, a half mile below town, where I took out, for a while, fifty to a hundred dollars per day. I also found good mines in Kelsey's Canyon, in which the gold was mainly flaxseed-shaped and of a very uniform and beautiful variety. The largest piece I ever found was in a gulch in the hills westward of town. Here, with the first stroke of the pick, I raked out of the clay an ounce chunk. With the next stroke, one weighing two and a quarter ounces. This was certainly encouraging for a beginning!

Mining Camps

Mining camps were usually hastily built, for the miners wanted to spend every available minute digging or panning for gold. Some of the miners took time to cut down trees and fashion crude log cabins. Others slept in tents they had brought with them.

Camps usually sprang up wherever a lucky miner found gold. When word of a good strike reached other miners, they flocked to the new camp. When the gold was gone, so were the miners, following rumors of gold to be found in other places.

Many mining camps had striking names: Hangtown, Grizzly Flats, Cool, Ben Hur, Placerville. Here miners could sell their gold, buy supplies, see friends, maybe even receive mail from friends and family back East.

Life in the mining camps was often rough. Fights broke out between miners if one thought that someone "jumped his claim," or took it over. In the earliest mining camps, the men made their own laws and enforced them by hanging offenders or chasing them out of camp.

Mining camps had a unique mixture of people. One writer wrote about Coloma, "The principal street was alive with crowds of moving men, passing and repassing, laughing, talking." In the crowd he saw African Americans, Jamaicans, Hawaiians, Chinese, Germans, Italians, Peruvians, Frenchmen, Mexicans, and Americans.

But the beginning proved also to be well nigh the end. As a rule, mining even at that day could not, by any means, be reckoned a profitable employment. A lady who kept boarders in Hang-town, in the winter of 1849–1850, informed me that very few of her boarders paid or were able to pay. One man, who applied himself diligently, owned to me that he had not taken out as much as a quarter of an ounce on any day during the winter.

At the time of our operations, the original diggings, where the largest nuggets had been found and where stood several cabins, were entirely deserted. The notion during the winter of 1849–1850 was that higher up in the Sierra Nevada Mountains lay the "big lumps" of which flakes and other small particles found lower down were but the float of waste.

Many were the extravagant yet fully credited rumors whispered from friend to friend as to the pound-a-day diggings invitingly awaiting spring to open up their treasures.

Not to be left napping under such circum-stances, I was among the very first to break from camp in spring. On the South Fork of the American River I found a party of miners who had long been rolling out the pound chunks the whole winter long. That is to say, it had confidingly come to my ears that someone had affirmed that he had seen a man who had heard another man say that he knew a fellow who was dead sure that he knew another fellow who, he was certain, belonged to a party shoveling up the big chunks — or something to that effect.

By now, of course, I knew we had been hoaxed, for of all men the goldminer is proverbially the readiest *"to swallow gudgeons* [small freshwater fish] *ere they're catched, and count the chickens ere they're hatched."*

Moving On

I removed to Placerville to try my luck at a new diggings. Placerville was the first point in the mines reached on the principal overland route in the season of 1850. Early in July, a steady stream of emigrants began to pour into my camp. The first arrival was a party from my own town in Indiana, the Fowler brothers. They had made the journey from the Missouri River with an ox stream in ninety days. The rush that season was very great, and soon every avenue was filled with new recruits.

A more disappointed and disheartened lot of mortals could scarcely be imagined. They believed, as did many of the old-timers also, that the diggings had been worked out and that the whole country had collapsed into utter ruin. This gloomy outlook was further aggravated by the sickness, which at Placerville was owing largely to stagnant, polluted water. Our water was

I REMOVED TO PLACERVILLE TO TRY MY LUCK AT A NEW DIGGINGS.

mostly obtained from abandoned prospecting holes, of which the streets were full.

I was taken with typhoid fever several weeks prior to the first arrivals from overland. I did not recover so as to be able to work until this camp and the neighboring sections had become overcrowded with the newcomers. An ounce of gold was the usual fee for medical attendance.

In the latter part of August, my friend William Good, with whom I had set out from Indiana over a year ago, arrived in Placerville from the Trinity diggings. He had come to this congested labor market to employ men to haul goods to northern camps. He engaged me and thirty others at three dollars per day and board. When we were going up the Sacramento Valley the fall before, we had met hundreds of men coming from the Trinity mines, cursing the diggings as utterly worthless. Yet, as a matter of fact, the yield there was about as good as anywhere else in California. Thus we found it everywhere, some coming, some going, some praising, some damning.

I accompanied Good, driving an ox team as far as Shasta, which was the end of the wagon road. This was but a few miles from the scene of my first mining attempts at Redding's Diggings.

We now had to pack the rest of the distance, some seventy miles to the head of Big Canyon on the Trinity River. Upon arriving I at once struck ounce diggings on a sandy bar near the river's edge. One afternoon I scooped up eighty dollars of gold in fine scales.

The Trinity River abounded in salmon. Every morning I saw a school of them. The fish were easily caught by the gills and tail with the hand. I thus supplied myself with a superabundance of this poor man's meat.

In the course of two months, the approach of winter caused an almost total abandonment of the Trinity diggings. One day, I went down through the canyon to the Big Bar. This had been the largest mining camp on the river. Now I found it totally deserted. Utensils and tools were strewn about the brush shanties as if the occupants had fled in a panic. Weaverville was the only camp nearby that bore any semblance to a town, and this is where everybody flocked who intended to overwinter in that region.

I followed the crowd to Weaverville.

Here, about a mile from town, between Ten-Cent Gulch and East Weaver Creek, I put up for myself an eight-by-twelve log cabin with a generous chimney. The mountain lions were very numerous in the vicinity as their nightly serenades kept me constantly reminded. But with my strong door securely pinned, I felt amply assured against any undue intrusions on their part.

I did meet one of their lordships on a trail. I hardly need add that I was quite ready to yield him the right-of-way had he not, through his superior nimbleness, extended to me that courtesy first.

The camp was by no means a live one so, toward the close of winter, I moved back to the Trinity River, where I found the diggings pretty uniform and fairly good. Some claims paid an ounce a day [sixteen dollars] for hard work, but the average per day to the man was perhaps not far from ten dollars.

I remained on the Trinity until sometime in September 1851, when a recruiting officer appeared along the river enlisting volunteers for service against the Indians under a call issued by the governor. The miners of that region had no very warm attachment for either the Indians or the diggings. Most of them were ripe for anything that promised a change.

About sixty men, myself included, responded to the call. No more gold digging for me. I set forth as a soldier now. Bidding a not-over-tearful adieu to the diggings, we set out upon the extremely rough trail across range after range of mountains for Uniontown, on Humboldt Bay, a distance of some ninety miles.

We did not find things altogether to our liking after our arrival. After staying in camp for several weeks with no prospect of being enrolled into the militia, we disbanded. My careers in mining and soldiering were now at an end.

I became a woodcutter again at Uniontown (now Arcata) that winter of 1851. The town lay immediately at the edge of the great redwoods, the finest forest in the world. The timber yielded readily. Using my boyhood lumbering skills, I was occupied during most of the winter getting out siding, for which I received ten cents apiece. I made about one hundred pieces a day.

The lumber industry was being rapidly developed. No less than seven sawmills were put into operation within a year. Eureka was the principal seat of this activity and to there I went. I would find my fortune in the riches of the redwoods.

The mills buzzed away day and night. The

woods resounded with the sound of the logger's ax. Everybody was busy, everybody had money, and everybody seemed contented and happy. Each logger had his own timber claim and his own outfit. Mine was Leeper, Liles and Company.

There are no more impressive trees in the world than the redwoods. A redwood forest is a place where silence itself might feel the need of going on tiptoe. Fancy going mile after mile through trees 150 to 300 feet high packed as closely as trees can conveniently stand.

But the size of these redwood trees, their number, their grandeur, their immovably rooted bases, their beauty, their litheness, their remarkable straightness, none nor all of these are anything like so impressive as their age. They are nine hundred to fifteen hundred years old.

When I first looked upon these wonders, I was actually spellbound. Their huge, shapely columns, planted thickly about me, seemed to shoot up to the skies.

Of course, though their life is reckoned by the roll of centuries, yet they have their appointed cycle of years. It is truly sad to contemplate their majestic forms lying prostrate upon Mother Earth.

These giants seem to lose their footing more frequently after the close of a storm than during its progress. Often, in the quiet following a storm, as I lay in my bunk, I would hear one after another of these mighty giants of the forest lose their hold and come tumbling down to earth. In its death agonies, each tree sounded as if it had brought down with it the thunders of heaven.

My Story Ends

Now I must bring my account to its end. My dreams of striking it rich in the Golden State had proven to be the gold of fools. Like so many others I had come to California for easy pickings and found myself working harder than I would have back home in Indiana.

With these thoughts I chose not to remain in California any longer. I sold my share of Leeper, Liles and Company. With the proceeds I purchased my ticket home. In April 1854, I sailed on the schooner *Sierra Nevada* for San Francisco. On May 16 I sailed for New York, via Central America, taking the steamer *Brother Jonathan* on the Pacific side and the steamer *Star of the West* on the Atlantic side.

The journey could scarcely have been more pleasant: fine weather, no accidents, no sickness, no deaths, good fare, accommodating officers, and agreeable passengers. Distance from San Francisco, 6,700 miles, making altogether a

ON MAY 16 I SAILED FOR NEW YORK, TAKING THE STEAMER *BROTHER JONATHAN* ON THE PACIFIC SIDE.

journey of over 10,000 miles and an experience of five years and four months.

I may now be permitted a few concluding reflections. In 1849, 42,000 gold-seeking Argonauts reached the goldfields by land and 39,000 by sea. In 1850, the rush hither was still greater and the stream continued to flow year after year. These Argonauts were for the most part under middle age and the degree of pluck and energy they displayed in this novel field has probably never been paralleled. They explored difficult and dangerous mountain recesses, upturned gulches and canyons, washed away flats and bars, turned rivers from their beds, tunneled mountains, sluiced away hundreds of miles of earth, built up towns and cities, developed agriculture, established courts of justice, and set up and put in motion a state government. In a word, they gave impetus to human progress throughout the globe to an extent never before equaled in the same period of time since the dawn of history.

The Golden State itself is truly a unique land with a unique history. Widely isolated betwixt desert and ocean from the great hives of humanity, it is a world of itself, and has built up a civilization in large measure peculiarly its own.

Yet it is not a world without its drawbacks. To me, surely, it did not afford an unceasing round of pleasure. Still, to me, as to most others who have once known and felt its peculiar fascinations, its mountains and valleys, its forest and streams, its fruits and flowers, its scenes, there is a charm, an indescribable something, that lingers in the memory like a fairy dream, which neither time nor distance can ever lessen.

EDITORS' NOTE

David R. Leeper was a fine writer. In editing his account, we sometimes shortened his lengthy sentences, a style of his time. Here and there we revised a sentence in order to make its meaning clear to the modern reader. We also modernized spelling and punctuation. Essentially, however, we have let Leeper tell his tale in his own words.

GLOSSARY

adieu (uh DOO) French word for "good-bye"

Argonauts gold seekers, named for Jason and his Argonauts, characters in Greek mythology who searched for the Golden Fleece

board food paid for by a lodger

chase hunt

cord stacked firewood measuring four by four by eight feet

diggings place where gold was found

emigrant a person leaving one place to settle in another

escarpment cliff

ford to cross a river in a shallow place

formidable challenging

Forty-niner nickname given to gold seekers who rushed to California in 1849

frontier a region beyond an area that is settled

geyser (GUY zir) a fountain of hot water

gradient slope of a mountain or hill

junket trip

lave to wash; to bathe

placer deposit of gold

plains level, treeless lands, often dry

prairie   grassland

redwood   a giant Sequoia tree

schooner   a sailing ship

scurvy   a gum disease due to lack of vitamin C in a person's diet

staple   major part of a person's diet

territory   a part of the United States not admitted as a state

virtuoso   (vuhr choo O so) a person skilled in an art such as singing

TO LEARN MORE ABOUT THE CALIFORNIA GOLD RUSH

NONFICTION BOOKS

Blumberg, Rhoda. *The Great American Gold Rush*. New York: Bradbury Press, 1989.

Johnson, William Weber. *The Forty-Niners*. New York: Time-Life Books, 1974.

Ketchum, Liza. *The Gold Rush*. Boston: Little, Brown, 1996.

Krensky, Stephen. *Striking It Rich: The Story of the California Gold Rush*. New York: Simon and Schuster, 1996.

FICTION

Cushman, Karen. *The Ballad of Lucy Whipple*. New York: Clarion, 1996.

Fleischman, Sid. *By the Great Horn Spoon!* Boston: Little, Brown, 1963.

Gregory, Kristiana. *Across the Wide and Lonesome Prairie*. New York: Scholastic, 1997.

———. *Orphan Runaways*. New York: Scholastic, 1998.

PLACES TO VISIT

California Historical Society,
78 Mission Street,
San Francisco, California 94105

Gold Bug Mine, Placerville, California
  Demonstration gold mine
Marshall Gold Discovery State Historic Park
  (eight miles north of Placerville on California
  Highway 49)
  Self-guiding trails with Marshall's cabin and grave;
  reconstruction of Sutter's Mill
Scotts Bluff National Monument, Gering, Nebraska.
  Oregon Trail Museum, Visitors' Center
  Tells story of Western migration, historical programs,
  road to the summit
Sequoia National Forest, 900 W. Grand Avenue,
  Porterville, California 93257
Shasta State Historic Park
  (six miles west of Redding, California, on California
  Highway 299)
  Gold Rush Center, museum, cemeteries

WEBSITES*

California Historical Society
www.calhist.org
California Home Page
www.ca.gov

*Websites change from time to time. For additional on-line infor-
mation, check with the media specialist at your local library.

INDEX

Page numbers for illustrations are in boldface